Prittlewell: A history.

By
M Sipple.

Prittlewell: A history.

**Published by;
JTT Publishing.**

All rights reserved. Copyright © 2008 Mavis Sipple.

No part of this book may be reproduced or transmitted in any form or by any means, graphic, electronic, or mechanical, including photocopying, recording, taping or by any information storage or retrieval system, without the permission in writing from the publisher or author, except in the case of brief quotations embodied in critical articles and/ or reviews.

ISBN 13: 978-1-906529-12-3

JTT Publishing books may be ordered through all internet booksellers, or through your local book retailer.

Printed in the United Kingdom.

Bibliography.

Peter Mason & David Goody; Official History of the Blues.
Burrows, J.W. Southend-on-Sea and District.
Gowing, Cannon E N. The Story of Prittlewell Church.
Pearce, Marion; Milton, Chalkwell, and the Crowstone.
Sipple, M. Rochford a History. Titbits and Tales of Essex Inns/Old Essex.
Southend Standard.
Williams, Judith; Leigh-on-Sea, a history.
Yearsley, Ian; A History of Southend.

Acknowledgements.

I would like to thank Barry Anderson, Bonnie and John Rogers, Ian Smith, Peggy Webster and Judith Williams, and all those who kindly allowed me to use their photographs. The staff at Southend library for their help, and the many people who have fed me snippets of information. Also, Pete, for his encouragement and computer skills.
The Essex Records Office for their kind use of the cinema plan, featured on page 78.

To Kathryn.

Contents.

The beginning;   9

The Priory	12
The Church	16
The Jesus Guild	19
Prittlewell Fair	22
The Parish	24
The Roads	26
Education	29
The Workhouse	32
Religion	33
Houses	37
Inns	48
The coming of the railway	55
Water	56
Crime	57
The New road to Southend	59

The 20th century;

The Prittlewell Improvement Scheme	63
R. A. Jones	66
Football	70
The Airport	72
The Priory Improvement Scheme	76
The Arterial Road	79
The Hospital	80
Expansion	81
Churches	84

The 21st Century;

Priory Park & 'Camp Bling.'	97
The Airport	100
The Allotments	102
A final thought ...	103

The beginning ...

There has been some kind of settlement at Prittlewell for hundreds of years. According to the Essex Book of names, Prittlewell means 'babbling brook'.

The Reverend Gowing is said to have traced the brook from source to mouth. He found it began as a puddle near Thundersley reservoir, nearly 300 feet above sea level, ran along Poors Lane, through Belfairs Woods, past Victoria Avenue, until it reached the fish ponds in Priory Park, then, it meanders under Sutton Bridge and joins the River Roach at Stambridge Mill.

Evidence of Bronze age, iron age, and Roman settlements have been found in the Prittlewell area.
Burial urns, tools, weapons, and pottery vessels from 50 BC to 50 AD have been discovered at Roots Hall, Fossetts Farm, and along Eastern Avenue.

The Saxons developed the Manorial System in England. The manor of Prittlewell was around 900 acres of land, its boundaries being, roughly, the coast in the south, around Chalkwell in the west, and Warner's Bridge to the North. They built the original village of Prittlewell, which was a small group of simple buildings.
One of their burial grounds was found on the east side of Priory Park. The method of their burials shows that they were pagans; they took to their grave anything they might need in the afterlife. By the 8th century they were converted to Christianity.

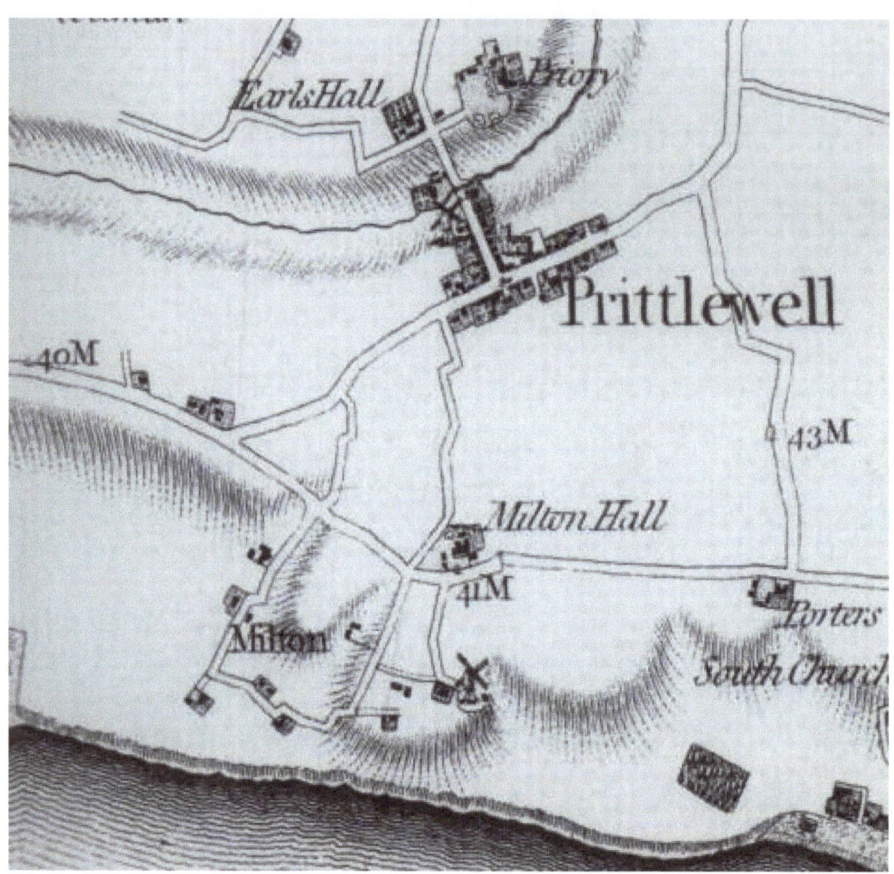

Prittlewell; 1777.

At the time of the Domesday Book, Prittlewell, then known as Pritte Wella was held by Sweyne (Swein) one of the few landowners who retained their property after William had assumed the crown.

Sweyne owned most of the land in south east Essex. He was the greatest sheep-master in Essex. He had over 4000 sheep on the marshes. It was Sweyne who built a castle in Rayleigh.

Swein holds PRJTfLEWELL in lordship for 71/2 hides.
   Then 7~villagers, now 4; then 14 smallholders, now 23. Then
     2 ploughs in lordship, now 3. Then 7 men's ploughs, now 9. Pasture, 12 pigs; pasture, 200 sheep. Then 2 cobs, 8 cattle,
     30 pigs, 1OO sheep; now 1 cob, 3 foals, 13 cattle, 65 pigs, 200 sheep less 4, 66 goats, 9 beehives.
   Of this land, 1 free man holds 1 virgate which he could sell;
but the jurisdiction lay in (the lands of) this manor. To (the lands of) this manor's church 2 men added 30 acres of another land. Value always £12.
   Of this manor, Grapinel holds 1/2 hide.
   2 smallholders. 1 plough.
Value 10s in the same assessment.

> Pritteuuellā. ten& .S. in dnīo. p̄. vii. hid. 7. dim. Tc. vii. uilt. m̄. iiii. Tc. xiiii. bord. m̄. xxiii. Tc. ii. car. in dnīo m̄. iii. Tc. vii. car. hōu m̄. ix. Past. xii. porc. Past. cc. ou. Tc. ii. runc. viii. an. xxx. porc. .c. ou. M̄. i. runc. iii. pult. xiii. an. lxv. porc. cc. ou. iiii. min. .lxvi. cap. ix. uasa ap. ⸗De hāc t̄ra ten&. i. lib hō. i. uirḡ quā pot̄at uende. f; foca jacuit in hoc manerio. 7 ad eccl̄iam huj manerij. appofuer̄. ii. hōes. xxx. ac̄. de alīa t̄ra. Sēp ual. xii. lib. De hoc Man ten& Grapinel dim̄. hidā. 7. ii. bord. 7. i. car. 7. ual. x. fol in eod p̄tio.

Prittlewell in the Domesday Book before Southend existed.

The Priory.

In the 12th century, Lord of the Manor, Robert de Essex, gave the manor of Prittlewell, and other land, to the Clunic Monastry of Lewes. Upon this land was built the Priory of Prittlewell. Robert de Essex used tithes from Eastwood, Sutton and Prittlewell for the foundation of the priory. The order was part of the Benedictine's, originally from Cluny of Burgundy. The monks farmed the land, maintained the bridges, repaired the highways, cared for the sick and looked after the spiritual well being of the villagers. The priory was a cell of Lewes Abbey and was ordered to pay, every year forever on the feast of St. Pancras, one mark of silver as a token.

There were usually only about sixteen monks at the Priory and they led a Spartan life. They slept in their clothes and were buried in the dress of their order. They believed that a man dressed as a monk would be received immediately into paradise.
It was around this time that Earls Hall and Chalkwell became manors, taking some of Prittlewell's land.
Soon after the Suppression of the Monasteries, the priory church and part of the monastery were destroyed. On June 18th, 1536, four commissioners of King Henry VIII visited Prittlewell and compiled a list of the contents of the priory church and every room and chamber in the adjoining buildings. All possessions were sold to the crown. On the suppression of a religious house, provision was usually made for the evicted monks, pensions were granted and paid and many of the brethren were found employment in other fields of religious activity. Prittlewell Priory received a grant of £20 pa.

In 1537, the remains of the priory, plus its woods, fisheries, land and cottages - also the whole church, the lead upon it and the cemetery of the former priory, all houses, stables, dovecotes, yards, orchards, gardens, waters, ponds, fish, lands and soil beneath the surface, were sold to Thomas Audley for £400.
Ten years later, there being no heirs to the Audley family, it was sold for £800 to Lord Rich. The lodge, cellar and refectory buildings were converted into a farm house. The Rich family also acquired Hadleigh Wood, and land in Eastwood, Hadleigh and Leigh.
In 1678, the estate became the property of the Earl of Nottingham and later the Scratton family and their descendants owned it, until the 20th Century.
In 1917, the house and grounds were again on the market and were bought by Mr. R. A. Jones, to stop the land being sold for housing. He converted the house back to its medieval state and made the 40 acres of ground into a public park. Mr Jones, a jeweller from Southend, known as 'the people's friend,' donated the park to the people of Southend.
Mr Jones and his son, E. C. Jones, are buried in the grounds of the priory.

The Priory.

Southend Corporation carried out some restoration work and changed the priory to reflect the time when the monks lived there.

The lake.

The Old World garden.

The Church.

Prittlewell Parish Church, St Mary the Virgin, dates back to Saxon times. There was no local stone nearby, so the church was built of Kentish ragstone and limestone brought from Lincolnshire. The building has seen many alterations over the years. The tower was built in about 1470 and the porch a little later. The oldest part of the church is the North wall, where there is a Saxon arch built of Roman bricks. The doorway in the west wall led to a room which was used as a schoolroom or priest's lodging.

Saxon arch built of Roman Bricks, on the North Wall, the oldest part of the church.

The Bells.

The church has ten bells. The three oldest bells date from 1603. Bells were traditionally given names, the tenor bell was made by John Darbie, when it was reset it was named after King Edward VII to commemorate his coronation. In the 1960's the bells were in danger of cracking so a 'save St. Mary's Bells' fund was launched. By 1968 the repaired bells were back in the belfry.
Bells have been used in Churches, Monasteries and Cathedrals since the 7th century, and were rung to call people to worship, to welcome in the new year, for notable land or sea victories, for celebrations, and warnings of disaster.
Prittlewell was always famous for its bell ringing. Ringers received payment of about 12/-.
One vicar, the Reverend Nolan, ruled that the Bells should be rung at 5 am.

> One parishioner wrote;
> *'Disturbers of the human race*
> *Your bells are always ringing,*
> *I wish the ropes were round your necks*
> *And you upon them swinging.'*

Reverend Nolan later tried to change the time to 8 am, as his house was next to the church and the bells disturbed his sleep, causing him great annoyance.
One June day, in 1840, the distraught vicar went into the belfry to remonstrate with the ringers, to no avail. In desperation he returned with a carving knife and tried to cut the ropes. The ringers objected and scuffles broke out. Finally, the vicar called the police to prevent the ringers gaining entry to the tower. His windows were broken night after night. Despite locks and bars the ringers managed to get into the tower by climbing over the vicarage roof. The vicar fired several shots at them. The police were called. Five culprits were cited to appear in court and were fined. One of them, James Beeson, refused to pay the fine. He was sent to the debtors prison in Moulsham for thirteen weeks. The parishioners made a collection to pay his fine, so, he was freed on condition that he did not harass the Reverend Nolan again. Songs and jokes about the vicar became very popular and an effigy of him in his surplice was burnt on 5th November instead of a guy.
The Reverend Nolan was the vicar of St. Mary's for 42 years. He died in 1861, aged 85, and a plaque to his memory can be found in the church.

The Clock.

The original church clock was on the north side of the tower. When it was renovated in 1913, another dial was placed on the south side.
During a raid in the Second World War, two highly explosive bombs fell near the church, partly demolishing the Hall. The two faces of the clock were damaged by shrapnel. They were taken to London, in 1950, for repair and for the gild to be replaced.

An article in the newspaper, in 1924, mentions that architect, Mr. Johnstone, was supervising the repairing of parts of the fabric of St. Mary's tower. He noticed a cross of black flints on the South east face. This is believed it to be a consecration cross placed by the builders to mark the completion of their work.
It is likely that the cross was blessed by the prior of the Clunic house, Prittlewell Priory. He would have dipped his thumb into the sacred oil and, tracing the cross, blessed it.

The Jesus Guild.

During the 15th century, the revenue of the monasteries had been in decline. Prittlewell Priory was so poor that the monks were barely able to help people in need.
Around that time, the Jesus Guild was founded in Prittlewell with both men and women members. The aims of the guild were to help care for the sick and needy, to educate the children of the parish, and to make sure those who could not afford it were given a decent burial.
Their own Guild priest helped with the education of the young. The guild played a significant part in the running of the parish for many years, taking care of the religious and social welfare of the community. They were responsible for the alterations made to the church, which was enlarged and restored. The members built the Jesus Chapel. The South Aisle was referred to in the wills of the period as the Jesus Aisle.

A guild house was built where members met for feasting and business meetings. According to local historian, J.W.Burrows, the Guild House was probably on the south side of the street opposite the church. There was a house there named the Jesus House. It was possibly the house later named Reynolds, which you can see below.
When this house was demolished to make way for the extension to the Blue Boar, a rare ancient fireplace was discovered. This huge fireplace is now in the Southend Museum.

(Above) West Street. The Blue Boar is on the left & Deeds Cottage is on the right. This was pulled down for road widening.

The previous image shows the present Guild Hall, in Hill Road, on part of Church Field. The former Hall was destroyed by fire.
The present hall was built by Southend-on-Sea Estates Co. in 1936; It was dedicated by the Bishop of Chelmsford, in Memory of
Prittlewell boy - and first mayor of Southend - Thomas Dowsett.

St. Mary's Hall.

Used for public meetings, coffee mornings & craft fairs. At the rear of the building is another large hall, fitted out as a snooker hall.

Prittlewell Fair.

At one time, around the 13th century, Prittlewell had its own weekly market. Hugh de Vere secured a weekly market but this had ceased to exist when mapmaker John Norden described Prittlewell as 'sometime a market towne.'
It is said that Prittlewell traded its market for the bells of Rochford Church, which Anne Boleyn, when she lived in Rochford Hall, found to be a nuisance.
Wealthy merchant, John Cocke, bequeathed 100 shillings for the building of a market cross. This seems never to have materialised.

Prittlewell Fair was held annually, on the 15th. & 16th July, alongside St. Mary's Church. Hundreds of people attended, there were stalls selling almost anything from toys, sweets and gingerbread, to bread and beer.
Gypsies and hawkers came from all around the country to take part. North Street was lined with carts, sheds and barrows. The pubs were open at any hour the publican chose. It was often a rowdy affair, fights frequently broke out as old scores were settled and new arguments arose. These fights often resulted in the 'rowdies' being confined in the village lock up, which was near the church, or in the stocks. Six or more constables were needed to keep the peace.

    In 1665, there was no fair, it was cancelled because the great plague was raging in London. The fair was not by charter, so therefore it could be closed. The great fear was that the plague could be spread to Prittlewell by the visitors coming to sell their wares.

    Dr. Asplins' diary records how, when he lived in North Street, the stalls were set out in front of his house. He mentioned a giant and a giantess, an Albiness from Baffin Bay, a dwarf, and a learned pig and punch.
Mr. John Perry told the Southend Standard, in 1924, that he remembered how the stalls were set up in North Street and West Street, to the Blue Boar. Penny sausages and a ha'penny bread were sold. Shows were set up on Goodman's Green (a space that opened out onto the south side of East Street.) The Spread Eagle had a booth outside in which dancing took place. Prittlewellers enjoyed gooseberry pie and new potatoes. There was dancing, games and cart racing. The pubs opened their doors as early as the publican chose and closed them at 11 o' clock.

    The fair was abolished in 1872. Daniel Scratton declared that it was unnecessary and the cause of great immorality and injurious to the people of the town. Mr. Scratton said he was willing to give up his rights to any tolls arising from the fair.

    He said; "I shall be pleased to know it is being done away with."

A petition for the closure of the fair was endorsed by Henry Garon, grocer, Henry and William Dowsett, boot and shoe makers, Arthur Bentall and the Reverend Wigram, Arundell Neave, Lord of the Manor of Earls Hall, and Daniel Scratton, Lord of the manor of Prittlewell Priory.

North Street, now named Victoria Avenue.

The Parish.

Shortly before the reign of Elizabeth I, the priory and the guild were suppressed and the parish became a district of civil administration. The parish was mainly agricultural, the part near the coast to the south which became known as the South End, was just a few fishermen's huts.

In 1642, parish registers were instituted, giving records of baptisms, marriages and deaths in the parish. The records were kept by the overseer. When the Overseer of Prittlewell kept the records he also wrote a short history of the registers, in the back of the book. One entry tells that, in1597, the thirty ninth year of Elizabeth, all entries were to be copied into vellum books provided by the parish.

In 1605, it was compulsory to send copies to the Bishop's registry of the Diocese. (Many of the Essex records were destroyed in the Great Fire of London.) Copies of all these records had, by law, to be kept in the parish chest, which was opened only when all three key holders were present. The book records the burial of Margaret Bush, from Temple Farm, who hanged herself and was buried in the backside of the church. The back or north side of the churchyard was considered to be the devil's side and was reserved for suicides, criminals, and those not baptised.

The book also records that John Pawsey, of Eastwood, was run over by a water-butt. There were several unknowns written as the 'walking people's child' or 'body thrown up by the sea' and a 'child left in a field near the Folly.'

After the 'Vexation Act' passed by Charles II, in 1678, the law was that, because of the decline of the woollen industry, all persons should be buried in wool to help the trade. Until then it had been normal to be buried in linen. The penalty for burying your loved one in a linen shroud was a fine. An affidavit had to be produced at the time of burial. The records report that some, like John Finch, were buried with no affidavit. This cost the family £5.

In 1665, at the third visitation of the plague, there were 14 burials, the next year the toll was 43.

It was quite common for the more wealthy residents to make bequests to the poor. In 1537, Thomas Cocke of Prittlewell left to the church; 'three bushels of wheat to be baked and made into penny loaves, a bullock to be killed and distributed to the poor annually at Christmas.'

Agnes Pry, who owned several properties in the area, bequeathed, 'to the Guild her second brass pot and six pewter vessels.'

Thomas Peck left all his goods to the family.

It reads; 'in the name of God, amen. I being in health and perfect memory doe make this my last will in the following manner. First I give to Mary, my beloved wife, £50 to be paid within a month. Also, to my dear wife, from the day of my death the lease to the parsonage of Prittlewell and all the profits arising from the said parsonage, from the day of my death to the expiration of the lease, she paying the rents. I bequeath to my sonne, Samuell all my coppiehold tennements in Prittlewell paying out of it to my sonne James £10 when twenty one years. I give my sonne Samuell my Hebrew bible, my greek testament and the large annotations on the English Bible, also the bedde, beadstead and green stooles in the parlour chamber, in the vicarage house in Prittlewell.

He also left his three other children £30 each, and to his brother, a doctor, a gold ring. This will was proved in June 1668.

Prittlewell Hill, looking towards the church.

The Roads

The main roads from Prittlewell were, North Street, leading from the church to Rochford, East Street, which took the traveller through Sutton Road to Porters, and West Street, this led to Milton and on to Leigh. A narrow track from the church led to Whitegate, later known as Victoria Circus, Southend.

It had been the duty of the Lord of the Manor to repair the roads, but, in the 16th century the responsibility for the main roads was transferred to the Parish. Two men were to become Overseers of the Highways. Every parishioner had to pay towards the cost. Maintenance of the smaller roads was left to the Lord of the Manor.

Richard Tabor, and some others, were taken to court for not 'scouring the road' from Prittlewell to Rochford, thus 'endangering the road from flooding.' Several men were sent to court for failing to send a cart, or team to help with road repairing.
Gravel from part of the beach, known as Arthur's Land, was used for repairing the roads until Mr Arthur, of Southend, refused to allow any more gravel being taken from his land.

There were frequent disputes between the people of Milton and those of Prittlewell about the responsibilities of the parish. The repair of the bridge over Prittle Brook being one of the main ones. The bridge was in great decay. Eventually, in 1800, a wider and stronger bridge was built, this was replaced in 1919. Some of the nearby cottages were demolished at the same time.

This postcard shows Prittlewell's main roads and the Priory.

North Street.

The photograph was taken, facing North, towards Cuckoo corner.

North Street, looking towards the church.

Education.

Part of the work of the Jesus Guild was to provide education for the poor of the village. It was the responsibility of the Chantry priest to teach the children, but, when the Guild was dis-endowed, at the time of Edward VI, the post of Chantry priest no longer existed. This meant that the children of the poor had little or no schooling for the next two hundred years.

In 1727, Reverend Thomas Case, Rector of Southchurch, who had once been the curate at Prittlewell, tried to organise some teaching for the poor children. He enlisted the help of Lord of the Manor, Daniel Scratton, who entrusted some land near the bridge in North Street, known as Glynds, and a small part of the garden of Mill Croft. (Mill Croft was at the time occupied by John Coles, schoolmaster.)

A condition of the grant was that the schoolmaster should teach ten poor children of the parish to read and write, and he should teach them the principles of the Christian religion. He had to pay a nominal rent and keep the school premises in good repair. Mr. Scratton later gave another twenty six acres and increased the number of children to be educated free to sixteen. The school house was built of lathe and plaster. The school room was about 20 feet wide and 30 feet long. The other rooms were used by the school master.

The school was later enlarged. In 1817, a brick built classroom was erected and this was used to teach the boys - the old building was used for the girls.

Children paid one penny a week to attend, except the sixteen boys paid for by the endowment. In 1836, the schoolmasters' salary was £23 a year and he also received £10 from the church collection and subscriptions from the parish. He was allowed to supplement this by taking private pupils in his spare time. His wife was to teach the girls but she received no wage. There were about 40 to 50 boys and 40 girls. The children started school at about seven years of age. They were taught reading and writing, and religious education. The girls also learnt needlework. Books were supplied by the trustees, they also gave a cauldron of coal each year.

The 1841 census shows the schoolmaster was Edward Rolph, who lived in the school house with his wife Caroline and their six children.

Old cottages being pulled down in the 50's. They were built in 1727 and were once Prittlewell School.

North Street.
The old school building is shown on the right.

By 1877, the Prittlewell School board was formed. Prittlewell's vicar, the Reverend Pegram, was its first chairman.
The national School was built in East Street.

St. Mary's school moved to part of the old Dowsett School, in Boston Avenue.

The Workhouse

The poor relief act of 1601 meant that care of the poor was no longer the responsibility of the church, but of the parish. The parish built a workhouse on the road leading from Prittlewell to Sutton.

Social reformer, Edwin Chadwick, arranged to have local boards of Guardians and Overseers to take on the duty of caring for the poor and elderly. The poor were kept in the workhouse for 3 shillings a head. Conditions in the workhouse were often horrendous. Residents were treated cruelly, wives and husbands were separated, children were not allowed to see their parents - except at Christmas, when a feast was prepared for them all. The men had to wear dark grey clothes of coarse cloth with a large P for pauper on the coat collar. Women and girls were also forced to wear dark rough clothes marked with a P and they were also issued with brown stockings. They were employed in spinning and carding wool. The workhouse in Sutton Road was extended in 1820.

The 1841 census shows 12 people living in the workhouse. Thomas Archibald, aged 25, was a coachman, the rest of the men were agricultural labourers. There were two children aged 2 and 3 years.

In 1830 the Board of guardians was abolished and care of the poor was taken over by local authorities. Soon after this, the Rochford Union Workhouse was built and eventually residents from surrounding parishes were transferred there. The old workhouse building was sold to the Scratton family and converted into several houses called Mill Hill Cottages, but usually referred to as Workhouse Cottages. These and the lock up were demolished in 1960. Flats were built in their place.

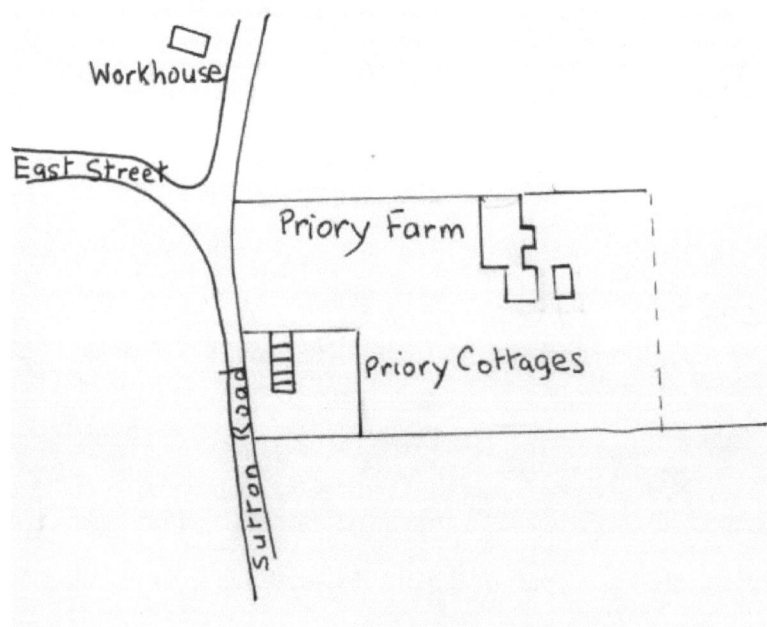

Religion.

Most people attended the parish Church and any kind of non conformism was frowned upon, but there were still some dissenters.

When a group of Congregationalists met at Rochford Hall, the Queen was informed and Lord Rich, owner of the Hall, was sent to prison. Despite the problems, small groups set up their own meeting places, usually in someone's house. Christopher Scott took out a licence to preach as a Presbyterian, meeting in a private house, as far back as 1672. Many others met in secret until the Toleration Act of 1689, gave them limited freedom to meet.

The Particular Baptists.

Famous Essex historian, Philip Benton, describes how the Particular Baptists had a chapel in East Street, Prittlewell, called the Providence Chapel. The chapel was built and endowed by John Sutton of Islington Green, in 1858, as a thanks offering to Anthony Smith.

Anthony Smith was a thatcher and gardener from Shopland. Mr. Sutton came to Southend for health reasons. One day, having taken a ride into Prittlewell, he stopped at the barber's shop and asked if they could tell him where the truth was preached. He then asked the same question at the shoemaker's shop. There he was told; "You will not find the truth in Prittlewell, but if you go to Southchurch, you will find a few poor people who meet in a room. One of the brethren speaks to them."

Mr. Sutton went to Southchurch to find these people and met Mr. Smith, a self taught man who was the preacher. Mr. Sutton was so impressed, he left eight half crowns in the collection and gave the preacher money to buy a good black suit.

The Providence Baptist Chapel, in East Street.

The Peculiar People

The founder of the peculiar People, James Banyard, was born in 1800 in a small cottage at Rochford. His father worked at Rochford Hall. James was a wild young man and he spent his time causing trouble, and frequenting rough and bawdy drinking houses.

His wife forced him to change his ways and go to church. He attended the Methodist chapel for a time but challenged their doctrine and eventually started his own sect, which met in a cottage in Rochford. The name was taken from the Old Testament; *'the lord has chosen you to be his peculiar people.'*

Banyard's preaching became so popular that chapels were opened throughout Essex. The first chapel in Prittlewell, on the corner of East Street and Penhurst Avenue, opened in 1850. There was also a chapel behind the cottages near the Golden Lion.

In 1848, the residents of Prittlewell were horrified at the death of a child. The parents, being Banyardites, had refused to call a doctor. The curate of St. Mary's preached against the parents and villagers sang anti Banyard songs.

When James Banyard, who preached in Rochford, called a doctor to his sick child, Many of the congregation took themselves to the chapel in Prittlewell.

The chapel in Wallis Avenue, opened in 1924.

Banyard was buried in the churchyard of Rochford church.

Houses

Probably the most famous house in the area is Porters, named after Lawrence le Porter, who held land in Prittlewell and Milton, in 1324.

Soon after the dissolution of the monasteries, Porters Grange was built, possibly on the foundations of an older building. The first known owner of the house was Humfrey Browne, who died in 1592.

There have been many owners of the estate, part of which was sold in lots for building. Porters and 29 acres of land were bought by James Heygate for £5,200.

The Heygates owned the property, until 1912, when the estate was sold for building, and Porters was to be pulled down. Fortunately it was saved by Sir Charles Nicholson, who bought it and lived there until 1932, when it was bought by Southend Corporation. By 1935, Porters became the Mayor's Parlour and Civic House.

Porters takes its name from the le Porter family, who owned much of the land in Prittlewell and Milton.

Bridge House

Bridge House, opposite Priory Park gates, was built in the mid 1700's on the site of a previous house. It was once part of Harp Farm and was used for a time as a tannery.
In 1965, it was bought by the council and it was decided that this Georgian property was of sufficient historical interest to be saved from the developers.
The Southend Standard reported, in 1966, that Bridge House was to stay, being the only Georgian building remaining intact, and it ought not to be demolished.

The house was neglected for some time and, with the help of vandals, became beyond rescue. In 1970, it was decided to sell it to the ministry of Buildings. The site was to be developed as a medical centre and driving test centre. The test centre was to replace those in Rectory Grove and the London Road.

In 2008 there were plans to relocate the test centre to Basildon. There had been a great deal of opposition to this scheme. The Driving Instructors Association spokesman said they would fight this decision as it would mean travelling long distances - and the cost of lessons would be doubled.

Colemans Farm

In 1553, the farm house and its 120 acres of arable land, were owned by the Colemans family.
By 1622, the farm belonged to the Earl of Warwick.
The house was demolished in 1970. Colemans stood near Southend hospital, which was built on part of the farm's land.

Earls Hall

When the Manor of Earls Hall was referred to in the Domesday Book, it belonged to the De Vere family.

Later, it became the property of John Vassal, a city merchant who is said to have sent ships to the Spanish Armada, and to have been part owner of the Mayflower. By 1841, the census shows James Tabor living there. Tabor owned Rochford Hall and several other grander houses, but he preferred to live at Earls Hall.

In 1889, an auction was held to sell off James Tabor's furniture, which included
mahogany and iron bedsteads, mattresses, quilts, Brussels and Turkey carpets, a mangle and two well built broughams, sets of harnesses, and lawnmowers.

Later, Earls Hall Farm belonged to Percy Bentall. When he died, his executors applied for permission to build several blocks of flats on the land. In June, 1963, the Southend Standard reported that planners had decided to leave this lovely ancient house for the present owners to live in, and its five acres to become a public open space.

Shortly after this, at an auction held at the Victoria Hotel, it was sold to the council for £85,000. They planned to build over 100 flats on the site.

When the house was demolished, the workmen found a 17th century floor and a 14th century fireplace, in the servants' quarters. Plans went ahead for the building of Cecil Court. The twelve storey block of flats, with 34 garages, were built by John Laing Constructions.

Part of the wall. All that now remains of Earls Hall.

Harp Farm

Harp house was situated near where the airport now stands. The Roundabout has recently been named Harp House Roundabout.

In 1723 Thomas Rogerson, of Bungay, Suffolk registered his name at a tenement called Harpes, with its outhouses, land and appurtenances in Eastwood and Prittlewell. The yearly rent was £10.

Benton mentions Harp Farm as being at the end of Love Lane, on the road to Rochford, and belonging to George Wood, solicitor of that town, who purchased it in 1827.

Iron age pottery and medieval pots were found on the site of Harp Farm.

Milton Hall

Milton Hall was originally owned by the monks. All tithes from the hamlet of Milton were paid to the priory at Prittlewell.

The Hall was bought by Lord Rich of Rochford, and later by Daniel Scratton. He sold the land for housing. The hall itself went to the Rev. Wannacott, he turned it into a private boarding school. The school lasted only a short time and the Reverend sold the hall to the Sisters of Nazareth.

Over the years the building has been altered and enlarged and, in 1900, the hall was demolished and a new convent, Nazareth House, was built in its place. This became a home for destitute children and the aged. Abandoned children were frequently left on the doorstep to be cared for by the nuns. Unwanted babies were placed in a metal cradle in the wall and a bell was rung to alert the nuns. They then took the child in and cared for it.

It is currently a home for the elderly.

Roots Hall

Originally called Rowards Hall, Roots Hall stood in 4 acres of ground, north of West Street.

By 1792, it was owned by John Kemp, then Michael Steward and later his son-in-law.

Benton said that 'portion of the land at Roots Hall, where the mill stood, belonged to Mr James Watson, miller, who was killed in a Great Wakering street, in 1843. It was later the property of Hugh Rankin, who sold it to Mr. Wigram, father of the present vicar.'

In 1876, the property was bought by Daniel Gossett and he sold the land in 1899. The house was demolished and the site became playing fields, used mainly by Prittlewell Cricket Club, and later Southend Football Club.

Drawing of a stock mill, built at Roots hall, around 1800.

Temple Sutton

In the 13th century, Temple Sutton was held by the Knights Templar. The Knights Templar were first formed in Jerusalem and their headquarters was in a building adjoining Solomon's temple.

The knights were a fierce military order of crusaders. By 1280, they owned a hospital, and 72 acres of land, in Prittlewell and Eastwood.

Ten years later, they owned land in Rochford and Sutton, totalling 100 acres. They were suppressed, in 1312, and their land was given to the Knights Hospitallers.

By the mid 1500's, it was owned by Lord Rich.

Two hundred years later, it belonged to Sir Richard Child and then to James Tabor.

The site of the old house is now Temple Farm Industrial Estate.

Temple Farm was situated on Sutton Road, just north of Fossetts Farm.

Sutherland Lodge

Once named Blue House, Sutherland lodge was once part of a farm.
This elegant house dates back to around 1600 - it was once a school.
The house was renamed when it was thought to be haunted, and difficult to sell.

Prittlewell Vicarage

The first vicarage was a small cottage, by the church. It was formerly part of Harp Farm, Eastwood.
This was moved to the other side of the road and the school built on the site.
The later, large vicarage, is on the corner of Shakespeare Drive and West Road. It was demolished around 1966 and housing built in its place.

The present vicarage is in Victoria Avenue.

The Inns

In 1592, it was reported that Prittlewell had nine alehouses adding ' fewer would serve we think.'
By 1692, there were seven inns listed; The King and Queen, the King's head, The Cock, the Red Lion, the Three Horseshoes, the George, and the Blue Boar.

The King's Head was where St. Mary's road is now. Further along the road was the Fox and Hounds, frequented by the bell-ringers. When Cannon Reay bought the King's Head, part of it was sold to the corporation and the rest was given to the church yard project. Travellers at the King's Head used to carry their own pad for sleeping on and a can for drinks. The boundary of the part they were permitted to use was marked by a wall and was known as the 'Paddy Can.'
Underneath the King's Head, traces of an ancient building were found, probably Tudor, with a spiral staircase and walls as thick as the church.

The Spread Eagle (above) was the venue for many important meetings and at times used as a court room. It also operated a carrier service taking coaches to Aldgate in London every Thursday and Saturday. This later became a weekly service. Jessie Payne, in her 'History of Southend' tells that the Spread Eagle was the venue for cock fighting between the gentlemen of Great Wakering and the gentleman of Prittlewell.

The Bell

The Bell, situated on the A127, was built around 1936. The great gold bell has been removed and the old sign taken down. The Bell now has the Toby sign outside.

The Blue Boar.

The sign is probably taken from the crest of the de Vere family, of Earls Hall. It had its licence as early as 1676. In 1841, Samuel Bragg was innkeeper, by 1901 it was owned by Frederick Garon. The Blue Boar, Prittlewell's oldest pub, was at one time the local telephone office. The early tram route passed the Blue Boar about that time.

Southend United Football Team was first planned at the Blue Boar.
In 1984, the 300 year old Blue Boar's name was changed to *Reids*. There were many objections to this. The landlord said that the corner was an accident black spot and that it was giving the pub a bad name.

Bottles from the Blue Boar Public House.

The Golden Lion (left) became empty in November 2008, the day after two fires broke out in empty rooms. The building was severely damaged.

The Railway Public House.

Bottles marked with 'Railway Hotel, Prittlewell.'

The Nelson Public House.

Two bottles stamped with 'Nelson Hotel, Prittlewell.'

A jug, from F.W. Davison & Co.

The coming of the railway.

The railway came to Prittlewell in October 1889. The first train for Rochford, Rayleigh, and London, left the 'elegant and spacious Great Eastern railway Station' in Southend, at 7.15 am.
A great celebration was held in Rochford, crowds turned out to see the first train, but, at Prittlewell 'its arrival did not cause much perturbation in any of the natives'.
There were just half a dozen people congregating on the platform and about a dozen on the bridge.
In 1907 there was a move to rename the station. The suggested name was Roots Hall Station. The idea was met with disdain from the locals.

Water

The pump stood at the bottom of the hill, by the bridge.

The original well is thought to have been in one of the ponds in the park and another was in the vicarage grounds. The main well was at the bottom of the hill by Glynds tenement. There was another at the top of the hill outside the Blue Boar which caused much aggravation amongst the residents, who declared it was a nuisance - it being in the middle of the road and dangerous. Finally, it collapsed, was covered up and therefore 'caused no more annoyance.'

The old village pump (left) can still be found outside the park gates.

Crime.

The Quarter session shows some of the offences against the law. The most common were selling beer at less that a penny a quart, not attending church, and trading without being apprenticed.

Three men were charged with having set free a man who had been put in the stocks by the constable. Francis Okey set the prisoner free and, when the constable tried to charge him, Okey's friend, James Clover, assaulted the constable.

Henry Gilliott, a shepherd from Prittlewell, and his friend Thomas Fairhead, who ran a butcher's shop at the back of the Old Ship in Rochford ,were caught stealing sheep. They were tried, found guilty and were hanged on the scaffold at Moulsham Street, Chelmsford, in 1820. They were the last men to be hanged in England for sheep stealing. Gilliott, who was just 24, had been married for just one month.

In 1894, the town was shocked when the body of Miss Florence Dennis was found in Prittlewell Brook. She had been shot through the left temple. Miss Dennis was pregnant by her murderer, James Canham Read. She had met James, a clerk, who worked at the Royal Docks, and didn't know he had a wife and eight children living in Stepney. The couple were seen together the day before the body was discovered. Concerned that Florence had not returned home, her sister rang Read to ask if he knew where she was - he denied having seen her. He then disappeared, taking with him £150 staff wages. He was traced to a house in London and arrested. The inquest took place at the Spread Eagle. Read was found guilty of 'shooting her through the temple by means of a pistol bullet, and killing her.' He was sentence to be hanged.

Superintendent Hawtree had a horse and trap waiting. Crowds gathered as Read, covered with a blanket, was driven to the police station in Alexander Street. Florence was buried in an unmarked grave in the north east corner of St. John's Churchyard.

Superintendent Hawtree.

The New Road to Southend.

While Prittlewell carried on in its usual, unhurried way, nearby Southend was becoming more and more popular. Bathing in the sea and healthy fresh air attracted visitors, and a number of houses were built. A coach service ran from Southend to Rochford, and then on to London.

Southend was still governed by Prittlewell but, by the late 1870's, the Southend Local Board had taken over the parish of Prittlewell and a new road was constructed, to connect Southend to Prittlewell.

The road - called by Mr. F. Wood, chairman of the local board - 'the New Road to Prittlewell 'was officially opened on Saturday, June 1st, 1889, and named Victoria Avenue, to celebrate the Golden Jubilee of Queen Victoria..

The cost of making the road was £4959 (16s, 9d).

According to the Southend Standard, members of the board met at their offices in Alexander Street and drove in three carriages, followed by Mr. Cogill's mineral water van, itself drawn by three horses and decorated with ribbons.

At the front of the procession rode Superintendent Hawtree and Sergeant Page. When they arrived at the new road, Mr. Wood stood in his landau and declared the road 'one of the finest developments in the county' open.

The next day, Sunday, members of the Salvation Army marched to the centre of the road, knelt and asked for divine blessing thereon and asked God to bless the people who lived on either side, and those using it.

Victoria Avenue, looking towards the church.

Victoria Avenue, looking from the Blue Boar towards Southend.

North Road Cemetery.

Sutton Road Cemetery.

By 1895, part of Jordons Farm in Sutton Road had been bought and consecrated. The new burial ground opened in 1900.

The 48 ½ acre ground is the resting place of many notable locals; the founder of the NSPCC and the founder of the Southend United football supporters club, to name but two.

Almshouses.

Prittlewell man, generous benefactor, and the first Mayor of Southend; Thomas Dowsett, built eight Almshouses in Chelmsford Avenue, in memory of Queen Victoria.

The 20th Century.

The Prittlewell Improvement Scheme.

By 1918, The Prittlewell Improvement Scheme had begun. This was to improve the area around the church. It later became known as the Prittlewell Memorial Scheme to remember those killed in the war.

At one time, the church was surrounded by shops. It is thought that roving players, travelling around performing mystery plays, set up small sheds on land in front of the church when they were performing. Gradually these were left on the site until the players returned the following year. Later they became permanent fixtures. When they were pulled down, human remains were found.

Benton says the churchyard was always a problem. Residents were responsible for anti social behaviour, leaving litter, drying linen, and grazing horses and other animals in the churchyard.

Finally, permanent shops were built on the site. In 1908, the vicar, Cannon Reay had bought a piece of land at the north west end of the churchyard, part of the site of the old Kings Head pub. Some of this land was sold to the corporation for road widening and the rest became part of the churchyard scheme. Travellers were allowed to use part of the area marked by a wall, to rest. This area was called the Paddy Can after the pad they used for sleeping on and the can they used to make tea.

When the building was demolished, a much older building was found with a Tudor spiral staircase, matching the one in the church tower, and walls as thick as the church walls - so the churchyard was built.

The Southend Standard, dated 1933, reports that under the improvement scheme, shops and houses on the corner of East Street and North Street were to be demolished, except numbers 3 & 5, whose owner refused to sell. The vicar of St. Mary's, Cannon Gowing, was keen for these improvements. St. Mary's would receive part of the site and £1,600, which would clear the overdraft of the improvements scheme.
The premises of Messrs S. Liddiard and Son were bought by the corporation and the land used for widening the road. Liddiard's well known pram shop was started by Frank Liddiard, in 1902, as a grocery and cycle shop. Liddiard built a new shop on the corner of St. Mary's Road.

The Lych gate at the church.

Memorial cross for those killed in the 1914-18 war.

R. A. Jones.

In 1914, Mr. R.A Jones presented the 15 acre Jones Memorial Ground to the residents of Southend, in memory of his wife, for use of the children attending elementary schools in the borough. This park and the priory were officially opened in 1920, by the Duke of York (later to become King George VI).
Local schools held their annual sports day in the Memorial Ground.

In 1917, Mr. Jones donated the Priory, and 30 acres of land, to the inhabitants of the county Borough of Southend–on-Sea, for perpetual public use.

The water fountain, presented to commemorate the glorious dead of the borough, who gave their all for Britain in the Great War.

Victory Sports Ground.

In 1921, Mr. Jones presented the Victory Sports Ground (above), in memory of the sportsmen who were killed in the 1914-18 War.

The impressive Jones memorial gates were made by Croxton & Son Vulcan Works, on Eastern Esplanade.

R.A. Jones died in 1925 and he presented Priory Park, Victory Sports Ground and Jones Memorial Ground to the people of Southend.

Liverpool born Mr. Jones was granted the Freedom of the Borough. His son, Cecil, also a generous benefactor, known as the shyest man in town, died in 1967, aged 82.

They are both buried in the grounds of the priory.

Football.

Roots Hall. The Southend United home ground.

There had been several football teams in Prittlewell before 1906, when, at a meeting in the Blue Boar, it was decided that there should at last be a professional Team. The team were to play at Roots hall, in West Street.

Mr. Ducal was to erect the grand stand of wood, holding 600 people, on the eastern side of the ground. The field was to be enclosed in a ten foot high fence and ropes would separate the players from the onlookers.

The ground was to hold a crowd of 6,000.

In July, an advert in the Standard read;

' Good free shoot for dry rubbish and earth. Southend United Football Club directors invite builders etc. to use the grounds of Roots Hall, Prittlewell, for the above purpose and thus making the embankments.'

The stadium was built of bricks from the Milton Hall Brick Company. Season tickets were available from Garon's Hairdressing Salon at 2 guineas for the stands and 12/6 for the grounds. The first match at the stadium was Southend V Swindon. Southend lost 1-0.

In 1916, the ground was converted to allotments to aid the war efforts. After the war the club transferred to the Kursaal. By 1914, they had moved to the Greyhound Stadium in Grainger Road, sharing the ground with the dog racing. This venue was unpopular with the spectators as the race track was between them and the players. By 1955, the team had returned to their former home of Roots Hall.

Ten years later, the Blues had debts of over £60,000. To help with expenses, they opened the new open air market with 400 stalls. The Shrimper's Club opened in 1967.

In 2008, plans are in hand to move once again, this time to Fossett's Farm. The sale of the site in Victoria Avenue will pay for the new stadium. Plans have been approved for a 22,000 seat stadium, a Sainsbury's superstore, 250 homes, a 114 room hotel, 127 flats, and retail space.
They promised that the market would be safe.

The Airport.

The airport was built during the First World War and, being self sufficient, it even had its own power supply. It was listed by the War Office as a potential site for a Royal Flying Corps Defence Aerodrome - described as a magnificent aerodrome a mile square. Several squadrons operated from there.

There were 11 fatalities during the conflict and by 1916, it had become a night landing ground. The first sortie ended with a Bleiriot having to make a forced landing on Leigh marshes.
Southend suffered several night raids. In 1915 properties were damaged, one person, Mrs. Whitwell, of North Road, Prittlewell, was asleep in bed when the raid took place. She was killed.
Several shells dropped on Nazareth House. Hundreds of bombs fell on Southend but Prittlewell remained remarkably unscathed.
After the war, 61 Squadron stayed at the airport until 1919. Then, civil aviation and pleasure flying began there. The airport was used for freight, passenger and joyriding flights.
In 1933, the council bought the site and Southend Airport was officially opened.
The Southend Flying Club first formed in a field in Ashingdon and moved to Southend Airport in 1935.
By 1940, and the Battle of Britain, the airport was controlled by the Royal Air Force. They played and important role in defending the country from enemy attacks.
There were several serious raids on the town; 15 bombs fell on Manners Way, demolishing the only occupied shop at Manners Corner. A bomb exploded in the gardens of houses in Hobblythick Lane, damaging several homes, and a number in Earls Hall Avenue. In Manners Way, the Boy's High School, suffered considerable damage to the building and the library.

Manners Corner was badly damaged.

The 1960's saw the heyday of the airport. BUAF (British United Air Ferries) carried Carvairs. (DC4's converted to carry cars.) Twenty flights a day left for Le Touquet, Ostend and Rotterdam. Fares ranged from £5. 4s. o.p for a single journey, and £9 per car.

Channel Airways flew Vikings, Dakota's, and Bristol Freighters. Flights left for the Channel Islands and the continent day and night. Nearly a million passengers used the airport every year. Tradair became a subsidiary of Channel Airways in a £33,000 deal. It made Channel the largest independent airline in Britain.
By 1964, a flight of Viscounts, able to travel at 400 mph, were in operation. The public flocked to the airport to be given a tour of the aircraft.
Later, a twin engined turbo jet, a Hawker Sidley 747, was ordered.

A Channel Airways brochure.

A Channel Airways Bristol Freighter, converted to carry cars as well as passengers.

The Golden Viscount, pride of Channel Airways.

The airport generated many related businesses: One, Lep Air, the first company to introduce air cargo services from the UK ,in 1953, operated from the airport, as did Southend Light Aviation Centre. They advertised 35 hour, private flying courses.
Air taxis by Executive Flying Services, Aircraft Maintenance companies such as Marmol Aviation Ltd., A.D.S Ltd., Aerial Spraying and fertilizing by aircraft, and several Travel Agents all operated from Southend Airport.

In 1967, the famous British Historic Aircraft Museum was opened. Advertised as Britain's most modern aircraft museum, it was open in the School holidays and weekends from 10am-5pm. Admission was 35p adults and 20p for children.

As newer and bigger aircraft were built, the runways became inadequate. The main runway needed to be extended, but this would mean demolishing some of the old cottages in Eastwoodbury Lane. There was great opposition to this plan. Finally, the government decided against the extension. The larger companies relocated. Channel Airways went into liquidation in 1972.

The Priory Improvement Scheme.

Work to improve the Priory began in 1938. The Council gave £500 for the work. This entailed demolishing the modern buildings standing in front of the Priory Church and clearing the ground between the Priory and Prittle brook. The area was turfed and the foundations of the church marked out so that visitors could visualise the church and monastic buildings. The improvements scheme was halted in 1939, at the outbreak of war.

The two carved fish, one halibut and one plaice, were discovered by Mr. L.A Huddart, who created the walled garden. He found the fish in a rubbish dump and rescued them. It was later found they had once been part of the pier entrance.

The old World Garden.

The Cinema.

Prittlewell's one cinema; the Star, opened in 1917. It seated 380 people and featured silent films. It was run by a Mr.Holloway.
The Star changed its name several times. In 1920 it became the Priory, later the Gaity, The Gibbs, then the Ideal, and finally The Picture House. When *'the talkies'* arrived, the Star, which had not been converted to take this new invention, closed down, in 1932. One of the last programmes was 'The Sheriff's Secret' featuring Jack Perrin and his horse Starlight; 'an attraction of the Western kind.'
The building was used for a variety of trades and finally became Physical City, which was pulled down in 1990. A block of flats now occupies the site.

Plan of the front of the cinema, approved March, 1915. The building was on two floors, had 3 rooms and an operating room. The brick built cinema was owned by Mr. W.C. Bradley. The architect was Chas. Cooke & Son, High street, Southend.

This building replaced the old cinema. The building was named Reynolds after the old house which used to stand near the site.

The Arterial road.

In 1920 the Great Arterial Road was being cut through the countryside. In 1921, the Ministry of Transport, the Director of Roads, and the Town Clerk all discussed the proposal to construct Eastern Avenue which terminated east of Romford, direct to Southend. The road was to be 100 feet wide and 21 miles long and was to be constructed in 6-9 months at a cost of £75,000. The road was officially opened in March, 1925, by H.R.H. Duke of Gloucester. (Prince Avenue is named after him.)

A procession of vehicles formed at Wanstead, to the borough boundary at a triumphal arch. Prince Henry was invited to cut the tape. A processions of cars proceeded to Southend, the 400 guests were invited to lunch at the Palace Hotel. The road went past the north of the park and cut through the Roman and Pagan cemetery. The bridge was widened and the road carried on to Hamstel Road. By 1929, the Council agreed that due to the great volume of traffic upon this road a second carriageway should be built.

The Arterial Road today, looking towards Cuckoo Corner.

The A127, looking west.

The Hospital.

The foundation stone of the hospital was laid, in 1929, by the Duchess of York, (later to become the Queen Mother,) before she married George VI.

The hospital was built on part of Colemans Farm.
M.P. Robert Guinness (later to become the Earl of Iveagh) donated the 12 acre site and £20,000. Cecil Jones donated £10,000 for the building of a children's wing, which opened in 1932. The proceeds from Southend carnival went towards fund-raising as well.

Lilies rising from a vase, the emblem of the Virgin Mary, were part of the seal of the Priory: this emblem is carved over the main door of the hospital. All trained nurses had the emblem on their badge. It was called the Prittlewell Lily. The lily was also depicted in the stained glass window in the chapel. The legend of the lily started at the time when the monks were looking for a place to build their monastery. They settled on top of Prittlewell Hill. However, the Abbot had a recurring dream in which he was told to go down to the fields by the river, there he would find Virgin Mary lilies growing. This was the place where they should build their monastery. They went to the fields, found the flowers and built the priory there. Later they built a small chapel on the hill. This is where the present St. Mary's church now stands.

Expansion.

PARTICULARS AND CONDITIONS OF SALE
OF
Nos. 2 & 3 Plumbs Yard, Westcliff-on-Sea.
No. 258, Hamlet Court Road, Westcliff-on-Sea.
No. 170, Westminster Drive, Westcliff-on-Sea,
AND
VALUABLE BUILDING PLOTS
ON THE
SOUTHBOURNE GROVE ESTATE
SOUTHBOURNE GROVE, WESTBOURNE GROVE, CARLINGFORD DRIVE, and MAIN ROAD.

EARLS HALL RISE ESTATE
MAIN ROAD, ROCHESTER DRIVE, and RICHMOND DRIVE.

PRITTLEWELL PARK ESTATE
OSNABURGH GARDENS, HOBLEYTHICK LANE, and CARLTON AVENUE, WESTCLIFF-ON-SEA.

Also Plots in ELMSLEIGH DRIVE, WOODLEIGH AVENUE, and EASTWOOD ROAD, LEIGH-ON-SEA, including

A FINE CORNER BUILDING SITE
in CARLTON AVENUE, WESTCLIFF-ON-SEA.

Also Plots at RAYLEIGH, ESSEX, on the RAYLEIGH STATION ESTATE, TURRET HOUSE ESTATE, RAYLEIGH PARK ESTATE.

To be SOLD BY AUCTION by Mr.

CLAUD W. DENNIS,
F.A.I.
In conjunction with Messrs.

ASHTON AGAR & Co.,
Ltd.

At the Hotel Victoria, Broadway, Southend-on-Sea,
On SATURDAY, 23rd NOVEMBER, 1929,
at 3 p.m. precisely.

Solicitors:—Messrs W. G. & S. BEECROFT, 49, Broadway, Leigh-on-Sea; Messrs. JOHNSON, PEACOCK, HEPWORTH & CHOWNE, 5, Grays Inn Square, W.C.1; Messrs. THURLOW-BAKER & NOLAN, Weston Chambers, Weston Road, Southend-on-Sea; Messrs. MARTIN & HASLETT, 7, Philpot Lane, E.C.; Messrs G. C. TOPHAM GREEN & Co., 5 & 7, Denmark Street, London Bridge, S.E.1; Messrs. VERNEY COOPER & Co., County Chambers, Weston Road, Southend-on-Sea; Messrs. MITCHELL, LUCAS & MITCHELL, 4, Romford Road, Stratford, E.15; A. S. BAILEY, Esq., 10, Promenade, Palmers Green, N.13; Messrs. PARSONS, EVANS & FRANCIS, 5, Cork Street, Bond Street, W.1; R. R. RAMUZ, Esq., 164, High Street, Southend-on-Sea; Messrs. DODSHON & HOMER, 126, Old Christchurch Road, Bournemouth.

Auctioneers:—Mr. CLAUD W. DENNIS, F.A.I, 58a, Newington Green, N.16; Messrs. ASHTON AGAR & Co., Ltd., F.A.L.P.A., 427, London Road and 5, Brightwell Avenue, Westcliff-on-Sea. Telephone 2624 Southend.

Plans of all the above Plots may be inspected at the Auctioneers Offices, 427, London Road, Westcliff-on-Sea, at any time before the Sale, or at the Auction Room, immediately before the Sale.

Wilson, Printer, Market Place, Alexandra Street, Southend.

The Churchfield Estate was developed in 1907, on land between the church and the priory. The Earls Hall Estate followed in 1930. A newspaper advertisement at the time described the Earls Hall Estate as being; *'Within walking distance of the Trackless trolley cars, motor buses pass every 15 minutes. Public services, gas water and electricity, shops and residential plots for sale. A considerable number have been sold and building has commenced.'*

In 1934, it was decided to erect a dozen shops to form 'a fine shopping parade at Cuckoo Corner.'
'This is an important entrance to the town and will present a remarkable chance to the first traffic roundabout in the district, made opposite the shops.'

Mrs. Queenie Anderson and friends, in the garden in Mayfield Avenue, in 1934. In the background are the roofs of the shops at Cuckoo Corner.

Cuckoo Corner in 2008, there are plans to create a roundabout here.
Soon after came the Manners Way Estate and another Road to Rochford.
A semi detached house on the Earls Hall Estate cost £750 or 19 shillings a week.
Loftus sun-trap houses with ideal boilers and all labour saving devices - and private garage-ways in Hampton Gardens, were on sale for £700.

Building the new estates led to the need for more educational facilities. The Church School in East Street was extended. (The school moved from East Street in 1999, to Boston Avenue, in part of the old Dowsett School.) In 1838, Earls Hall School was built. Wentworth boys and girls was built in 1946. Southend High School for Boys left the college building, at Victoria Circus, and relocated to the new building, in Prittlewell Chase, in the autumn of 1938.

Oaken Grange Drive, in the snow of 1987.

Oaken Grange Drive, in the hurricane of 1987.

The Churches.

The Congregational church in Chelmsford Avenue, opened in 1901. It was built and supported by the Cliff Town Congregational Church, but became independent in 1926. In 2006 there was talk of it, and three other churches, being demolished. By June, 2007, the church was advertised for sale, priced at £175,000. In November it was revealed that it was to become a mosque. It had been sold to the Essex Jamme Masjid Trust, which was based in Milton Road. The £1 Million deal included a block of flats which would be used as an Islamic Centre. The proceeds will go towards the redevelopment of the Church in Bournemouth Park Road.

The church Hall also included in the deal.

John Fisher R.C. Church, in Manners Way, opened as a temporary chapel, in 1939.

Earls Hall Baptist Church.

The present church opened in 1968. The original building on the site was virtually demolished, only parts of the east and north walls, and floors of the old building remain. The church first opened in 1942, with a membership of 39.

    The Hall was built on the site of a disused school.
The first caretaker, and a founder member, was Mr. Rutter. Mr Rutter was Prittlewell's lamplighter. His job was to clean the lamps during the day, light them at nightfall, and put them out in the morning. Mr Rutter provided his own tools and matches. His three mile walk round the town, attending to 90 lamps, brought him a wage of £1. 2s n 6d a week.

The Wesley Hall.

The Wesley Hall in West Road, opened in 1900 and the church opened in 1926.

In the 1970's the congregation dwindled. A Mr. Butt discovered that the church was about to close and, after a great deal of fund raising from all over the UK, it was bought for £16,000 by the UK Islamic Mission, in 1978.

St. Stephens' Church, Manners way.

During the second world war, the R. A. F. personnel were stationed at the airport. Many of them were billeted in the hall at the corner of Manners Way and Derek Gardens.

After the war, a large estate of prefabricated houses were built between Manners Way and Rochford Road. St. Stephens' Church was built to accommodate these newcomers to the area. The church acquired the Hall when it was no longer needed at the airport.

In 2006, there were plans to regenerate the area by building a new church and community centre.

The children's playground would have to be relocated.

St. Peter's Church, Eastbourne Grove.

The Bishop of Chelmsford created a new Parish. He dedicated the new church to St. Peter. The church In Eastbourne Grove is of a modern design but keeps its traditional character.
The mosaic in the entrance hall was designed by Miss Carter, art mistress at Westcliff High School for Girls, and depicts the cockerel that crowed when Peter denied Christ. The two smaller mosaics, a fishing boat, a fish and the keys, were made by pupils of the school.
St Peter's cost £33, 000 to build.

St. Lawrence Church.

In 1100 AD, the founder of Prittlewell Priory granted to the priory the church at Eastwood. So, there must have been an even earlier church on the site. This may have been the present Norman nave.
The church has gone through many changes and has recently been threatened with demolition, or possibly being physically moved to a new site, so that the airport expansion scheme can go ahead. So great was the outcry, the scheme was abandoned.

St. Lawrence Church. (Above.)

This building, situated in West Road, between Tudor Road and Chelmsford Avenue, used to be Westcliff Town Mission Hall.

EKCO.

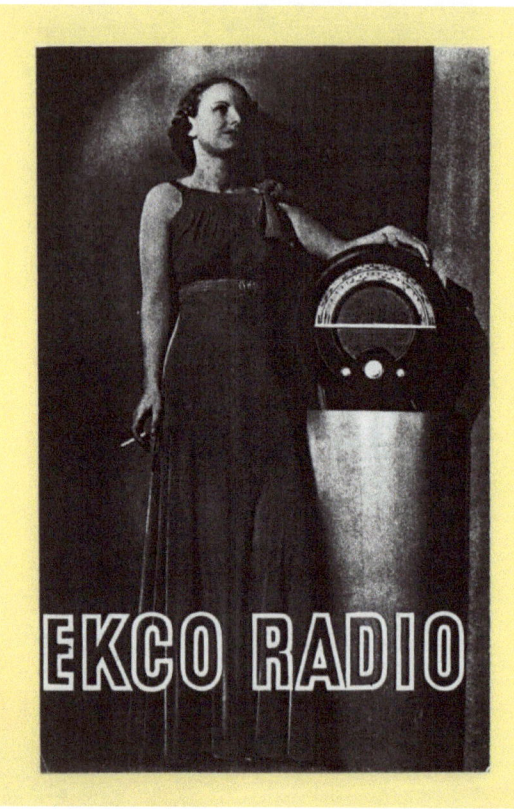

Eric Kirkham Cole ran a small shop, in Westcliff, selling radios and charging the old wireless accumulators. He and a partner bought a piece of land, opposite the north end of Priory Park, and built the Ekco factory there, making wireless sets, (originally out of sheet metal and later of bakelite.) They then made televisions as well.

They expanded the business to the Gliderdrome (the old skating rink in Southend) and Ekco Electronics Works in Ashingdon Road, Rochford.

By 1940, Ekco was one of the most important wireless making firms in the country. They went on to develop radar equipment which was invaluable during the war. Ekco Helicopter Radar claimed to be the most advanced in the world. The company employed 2,000 workers.

In 1966, Ekco merged with Pye. Later that year, because of the slump in sales of radios and TVs, 800 people were about to lose their jobs. Some were given four weeks notice, some were transferred to Lowestoft.

By 1984, Ekco and its 732 workforce were advertised for sale in the financial Times. Two years later the company was sold to Morganite Electrical Carbon. Ekco Plastics continued at part of the Priory Crescent site and gained awards for producing high standard work. The building was used by *Access*, (*your flexible friend*) and later Signet, the country's largest independent Financial Processors. Various banks had offices in the old Ekco building, before it became empty and derelict.

The old Ekco building in Priory Crescent.

The old Ekco building was pulled down in October, 2008. It was more economical to demolish it than to pay tax on an empty building. During demolition, a vast underground shelter was uncovered.

Churchill Gardens.

The Gardens opened in 1966. Originally part of the garden of Mr. Scheerboom, the gardens were presented by an anonymous donor, in honour of Sir Winston Churchill.
The gardens were opened by the Lord Lieutenant of Essex. A bust of Churchill, by Cyril Smith, was mounted on a wall in the garden. Sadly, this was stolen.
Before the gardens, the corner of Victoria Avenue and East Street there was a small shopping parade, with Garon's, Sopers, a photographer, a co-op and a chemist.

Prefabs.

Prefabricated houses, as shown in the photographs, were built as an emergency measure at the end of the Second World War.

1970 saw the few remaining prefabricated houses cleared from the site by Harp Roundabout. They had been built at the end of the war and were expected to last ten years.

When the site was due to be cleared, to make way for modern flats and houses, some residents refused to move. Some, like Mr. Clipson, had lived there for 25 years, and loved living there in the detached bungalow with its own garden. He refused to be re-housed in a small flat. The council decreed that the last remaining few must be moved by the end of that year.

The Old Bakery.

16th Century Deeds Cottages stood on the corner of West Street, and was demolished in the 1950's. Next to it was the old Carlton bakery.

The old bakery, standing on the corner of Victoria Avenue and West Street, was completely gutted by fire in 1998. Tree analysis found some of the timbers to have been felled in 1407, and the building erected soon after that, when the wood was still green. The bakery was an important building in its day, probably belonging to a merchant and possibly having a shop at the front. It was part of Earls Hall Manor. In 1619, John Wilkes sold it to Thomas Powlter. It was used as a bakery in 1801, maybe earlier. There was a large brick oven at the rear.

The building was under threat of being demolished, in 1962, when plans were afoot to build a roundabout at the junction.

Swan Hall was built when the old bakery burned down. Because this had been such an important building, it was decided to restore the hall to its original mediaeval appearance.

The bakery was the second oldest building in the town, the oldest being Warren's the butcher's, further down the road. A Mr. Warren, of Ilford, told a local reporter that the old house, once known as Warren's Cottages, was at one time a pull-up for coaches and at one time a hostelry. It had been tenanted by a family called Warran since 1800, and was later sold to Mr. Warren.

The Southend Standard, in 1833, reported that a ceiling had just been demolished in a room above T.A.Warren's shop, 13 North Street, Prittlewell, and access to an upper floor was revealed.

'From the frame of the house, it is undoubtedly to a 15th century domestic building. The frame is of oak and chestnut, the space between the studs is of wattle and daub. The building consists of north and south wings, and a central hall. The hall is open roofed, about 22 feet long and 13 feet wide. The roof timbers are blackened by smoke, suggesting an open fire for cooking and heating the building.'

A roadway had been made, possibly in the 18th century, through the hall.

Mr Warren presented an oak door, found in the north wing, to the Priory museum.

The Warren family ran a butcher's shop there for over a hundred years. More recently, the south side was run as a butcher's shop and the north side as Pippins the greengrocer. There have been several changes of ownership, but the property in now disused and for sale.

21st Century.

Priory Park & 'Camp Bling.'

In the early 1970's, there was talk of widening Priory Crescent, and making it into a dual carriageway through to Maplin, ready for the proposed Maplin Airport. This meant cutting through Priory Park and felling many of the trees. The park had been given to the people of the town, and the idea of losing some of it resulted in violent reaction from the public. Thousands of residents signed a petition against the road. A huge 'Save Priory Park' campaign began.

In 2003, the widening of Priory Crescent once more became an issue. Despite great opposition, the road widening was about to begin.

First archaeologists moved in and, amazingly, they discovered one of the most important sites ever found; the burial chamber of what was thought to be a Saxon King. The site, between the main road and the railway, was highly secret until it had revealed its treasures, which included glass jars, metal bowls, gold crosses, and a large belt buckle. The only human remains were tiny pieces of teeth. Among the most interesting artefacts were part of a musical instrument, thought to be a lyre, and some gaming pieces. The finds were taken to the London Museum and later returned to the Southend Museum, where they were on show to the public for a short time.

This incredible find put a stop to the road widening scheme for a time - but not for long. The council was determined to bury this unique site under a concrete road ... then the protesters arrived. They took up residence, built wooden huts, benders, a caravan, tree houses and settled in. The site, named Camp Bling, effectively stopped the road works.

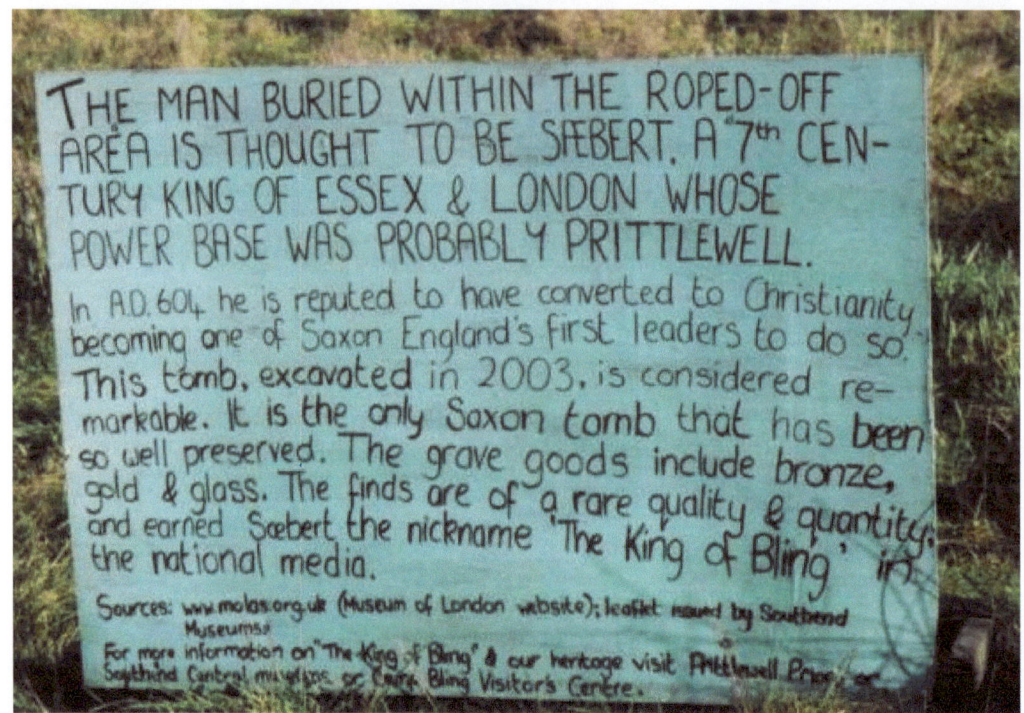

On January 18th, 2007 the Evening Echo announced that there was a possibility on the road widening idea being scrapped.

In 1999, the cost of the road would have been £3 million but the price had now risen to £21 million.

The Camp Bling residents stayed put, even after an arsonist attack. One Sunday night, one of the homes was set alight and the ferocious blaze caused the road to be closed as fire fighters fought to put out the fire, which raged through the trees, completely gutting one home. Councillor Garson's comment, according to the local paper was that he hoped they hadn't damaged the ground. Ironically, when the council were given an award for finding the Saxon site, their celebratory party was disturbed by locals trying to stop then from destroying the very site they had won the award for finding.

In June 2007, the local newspaper records that there was no hope, in the foreseeable future, of the road widening plans on the King's burial site to take place. But the road *could* be widened part of the way. This would mean felling 50 mature trees. Members of Parklife, the protesters, vowed to stay on the site until the road widening scheme had been scrapped. Councillors responded to the residents view by saying they wanted to safeguard and enhance the site of the Saxon King, adding, 'Protecting our heritage is our prime concern.'

The protesters and public were not convinced.

These weird cobwebs appeared on the bushes by the Site of the Saxon king.

The Airport.

The problem of lengthening the airport runway had been ongoing since the 60's. It is too short to take the large aircraft. In order to lengthen the runway, there was a plan to demolish St. Lawrence Church. This led to such opposition that it was abandoned in favour of taking off the spire and moving the church and graveyard 100 metres from its present site. This led to more complaints from the public ... even Prince Charles wrote to the vicar, expressing his dismay.

The perimeter of the church was festooned with yellow ribbons in a 'Save Eastwoodbury Church' campaign. An English Heritage spokesman doubted if the church could be moved. Finally, early in 2002, a solution was found; traffic lights and barriers were installed in Eastwoodbury Lane, closing the road to traffic when an aircraft was about to land, or take off.

Barriers across Eastwoodbury lane close the road to traffic when an aircraft is landing, or taking off.

By 2007, in a bid to get back into the passenger business, Southend Airport presented its new ten year plan to revamp the airport. It predicts 40 flights leaving or arriving every day, carrying over a million passengers a year and creating 1,000 new jobs. A new hotel with 130 bedrooms is being built on the old car park. There will also be a restaurant and a conference centre. The passenger terminal is to be modernised and a new control tower is to be built. The scheme should be up and running by 2009. There are also plans to build a new station on adjoining land.

February 2007; the airport is for sale. Improvement plans are to go ahead but the owners, Regional Airports, are hoping for a multi million pound offer. The Civil Aviation Authority has backed the elaborate plans to extend the runway - St Lawrence Church will not be moved, but part of Eastwoodbury Lane will be diverted.

The £12 million railway station has been given the go ahead and plans are to have it open by 2009. The latest rumour is that Eddie Stobart has made an offer for the Airport.

The allotments.

2006 was the year when the council granted permission for land by Warner's Bridge to be used as a cleansing depot, and waste transfer station. Despite much public disapproval, protest meetings, and petitions, the council was determined to go ahead with their plans. This meant that 17 allotments would be lost. Allotment holders were to be given three years free use of alternative plots and compensated for loss of crops. The site was to be fitted with CCTV cameras, a new car park, better watering facilities, a hut, and toilets. Residents still protested that the transfer station would mean more traffic and huge lorries turning in an already congested area.

This plan was finally abandoned in 2008.

A final thought on property in Prittlewell ...
and its future.

Manners Way Corner. A plan to add another storey on to the art deco building in Manners Way caused a great deal of consternation, and was eventually disbanded.

Six neglected garage sites were being sold for £1 each by the council. Garages at Lornes Close, Lincoln Chase and two in Derek Gardens will be demolished and affordable, rented and shared ownership homes will be built. The photographs on the next page show work beginning on this development.

Since I began this book several of the buildings have been demolished. How long will the following look the same?

The TA centre in East Street.

Ticket Office, once the army recruiting office, now for sale.

The Civil Defence Headquarters was built on the site of some old cottages. It was opened by Lord Derwent, in 1964. The building was taken over by the Royal Naval Association in the 1980's.

The corner of East Street and Station Avenue.

Shops on the corner of East Street and St. Benets Road.

East Street. On the right, the station, on the left, the Railway pub.

Shelford housing bungalows due to be demolished.

The Priory, Prittlewell's oldest building, has been allowed to become very run down. The first floor, housing the Prior's Chamber and Natural History Gallery, is considered to be unsafe, and has been closed to the public for several years. Happily, over £1million from the Heritage Lottery Fund is to become available. Friends of Southend Museums, and Cory Environmental Trust have pledged to match the grant. The building will be refurbished by 2010.